Selected Poems

PETER SANSOM has made 'a sort of living' as a poet for over twenty-five years. He has been Fellow in Poetry at both Leeds and Manchester Universities, and company poet for Marks & Spencer and Prudential. He is a director with Ann Sansom of the Poetry Business in Sheffield, where they edit *The North* magazine and Smith/Doorstop Books. His *Writing Poems* (Bloodaxe, 1994) has provided valuable guidance to many new poets. Carcanet publish his four previous collections: *Everything You've Heard is True*, a Poetry Book Society Recommendation (1990), *January* (1994), for which he received an Arts Council Writer's Bursary and an award from the Society of Authors, *Point of Sale* (2000) and *The Last Place on Earth* (2006).

Also by Peter Sansom from Carcanet

PETER SANSOM

Selected Poems

CARCANET

Acknowledgements

Poems are taken from the following collections: *Everything You've Heard Is True* (Carcanet, 1990), *January* (Carcanet, 1994), *Point of Sale* (Carcanet, 2000) and *The Last Place on Earth* (Carcanet, 2006). Much of the earlier work has been revised, sometimes to the point of being new poems.

The new poems here appeared in *Areté*, *Manchester Review*, *Poetry Review*, *Smiths Knoll* and *Stand*, and in a Rialto Bridge pamphlet, *The Night Is Young* (The Rialto, 2009). Many thanks to the editors, and especially Michael Mackmin. I would also like to raise my hat to the other pamphlet editors who have published my work over the years, the late Stanley Cook back in 1984, and John Killick, Geoff Hattersley and John Harvey.

I am grateful for an award from the Royal Literature Fund, and for a Fellowship at the University of Manchester during which many of the new poems were written.

First published in Great Britain in 2010 by
Carcanet Press Limited
Alliance House
Cross Street
Manchester M2 7AQ

A CIP catalogue record for this book is available from the British Library

ISBN 978 1 84777 064 6

The publisher acknowledges financial assistance from Arts Council England

Typeset by XL Publishing Services, Tiverton
Printed and bound in England by SRP Ltd, Exeter

for Ann

Poem

It was assembly and *Kes*, *The Loneliness*
of the Long Distance Runner, a window
onto winding gear at Teversall; and then
it was you
to contradict it with your glamour:

all public school and sixties London, you were
lessons outdoors one day-on-day of summer;
tennis after school and after tennis
the shower I watched you in; you were
the school play you wrote yourself

with me the lead. My writing took your slant,
your Greek e's and buckled y's.
You drove a minibus of us to France
and made *Paradise Lost* hilarious.
You were cynical and believed in us.

Then there was when it was *just* us,
the theatre or golf, jazz or Mozart round at yours,
and the afternoon you let me take the wheel
of your pride and joy
powder blue Volkswagen Beetle.

What you offered those days in good faith
has taken me this far, not far I know but far
for a boy going nowhere, till now
I have the means to write this at least – at last –
from wherever I am to wherever you are.

Contents

House

Half-three. Mum's at bingo
so the house is quiet. Joss is asleep
with his hand covering his face
from the light or from view.
The clock ticks either side of his breathing.

There's nothing in the paper
though the headline is 'Fish for Free'.
The dolphin thermometer
from Marineland, Scarbrough, breaks surface
in the shine on top of the telly.

The fire's built up but the room's cold.
Out of the window is the weather.
Dad comes in from upstairs,
the blood on his collar
is where he's been shaving

for tomorrow or the day after
if they haven't a bed. 'There's Half-pint,' he says,
'back from the gardens.
Nice clump of beetroot that.'
He presses his hand against the glass

and I see us for a moment on the allotment,
my foot on the too-heavy spade
pushing into October soil.
'I'll be off then,' I tell him,
'take the barrow down for the winnings.'

Snookered

Dad nods in the straight chair and me and Mum
are down to shandy. It's less and less likely
Jimmy White will stop Davies now. Midnight
when our Steve knocks, black from bagging up since dinner.

He's brought another hundredweight. Davies
puts another frame away while me and Joss
help him get it in the coalhouse. He stops for a fag
and a can of mild, and laughs when Davies

misses a sitter. 'Mr Interesting,' he says.
It's tense. Jimmy can't let this one slip.
Next door's phone goes – it should be disconnected
and when it stops I picture a white hand

lifting the receiver. We groan. Now Jimmy
needs snookers, and sure enough Davies sinks
the last red. Right, says Steve, but he sits back down
when the cue ball travels three angles to go

in off. 'The start,' he says 'of the biggest comeback
since Lazarus.' Nice, but we've heard it before,
and we'd have to see it to believe it.

Bingo

The stain on her finger like a bruise
told on her to the doctor,
a young man fool enough
to tell us in our own house
we'd not to smoke in here.

They'll just be going in at the bingo.
Dad's hands are jittery too
down the plaited wire
like a blind man to his cardigan pocket.
He turns the bevelled edge

like tuning a station
to what we're not saying,
and the hearing aid whistles.
He looks blank when we tell him
and sings about bluebells: bluebells are blue.

Mother shouts, 'You crazy mare,
switch that thing off.'
She holds the prescription tight,
like gripping a board with the winning card
two or three from house.

The Folklore of Plants

Joss slices hunks of ham
off the ham-hock. His hand clamps
the bone to the table
and he cuts away from himself 'because that way
you never cut yourself'. When he

eases the pressure, the milky pearl
of the knuckle shines more brightly.
I'm reading *The Folklore of Plants*.
It's Saturday tea,
makeshift, because Mother is poorly.

Blockbusters tells us the Italian-born pioneer
of radio was Macaroni. Dad grips the loaf
and butters the open edge before slicing.
Tea appears by magic
from under the rabbit tea cosy,

and I pour. Dave has given up sugar
but has to go in any case. His car-coat
half-on he looks helpless
when Dad says, 'You'll be blower-catched,
it's five-and-twenty past.'

So far no one's thought to ask Mother
if she wants a cup or anything to eat.
She's in bed again with the ulcer she kept
to herself for fear it was the cancer
that killed her sister.

Dave leaves and another brother comes in.
'Our Brian,' Dad says when he hears the door go,
but it's Tony. He has a big bunch of holly,
he doesn't say for Christmas
but for winter. He doesn't know

it's bad luck before Christmas Eve
(Mother wouldn't have it in the house)
and nobody says. 'Another book,'
he says cheerfully, shaking his head at me,
'you bloody live in books.'

Vacuum

The face and pate of a monk
and always wet-shaved to a blush.
Here to take the family to the sea
for the day, and by some anomaly

talking: explaining how a flask
keeps your tea hot or even Coca-Cola cold
to our Cynth's youngest. She listens
politely, but flinches from his kindness

when he goes to stroke her hair.
His hand is webbed with plaster
from glazing the greenhouse. For a moment
there's nothing to be done.

He looks round, an only son
to the aunt who's saying,
'Yes, they'll put the flags out
the day he gets married.' When he coughs

it's the bronny he's been off with
three painful weeks. He never took the tablets
and the doctor said they were
doing the world of good. At last

the sandwiches are done and stowed
with care in the huge beach bag. He stands,
suddenly a big man under this low ceiling.
But when he hands back the flask, he bends

beneath the tell-tale shingle-sigh
of broken silver glass.

One Night

One night I lay on my back in a field,
a warm clear summer night in the Lakes,
and looked up, with nothing better to do,
at the stars. And thought about matter
compacted to a pinhole of light,
and considered for the first time that I lay
with my back to a planet, and I named
the constellations that a friend's dad taught us
through binoculars in their back yard.
He took his own life, the dad, a hosepipe
to the exhaust in the middle of a forest.
I still don't know why. Maybe nobody does.
He enters my head tonight walking a lane,
a cold, clear winter night in the Lakes,
and I look up.

Funeral Morning

Another pot of tea at half seven and kick-off's
not till one. Another go with the sellotape
at the cat hairs so the trousers look ok.
Mum's put a button on the white shirt.
I won't be going beneath anyone. She means

our Chris in his uniform. He's in the navy,
was there when the *Belgrano* went down.
Half eight. They're delivering coal across the road.
The pullover is Brian's, 'just your sort'.
She needs to pee like a dressmaker, but Dad

won't put his socks on till she's cut his toenails
and we'll have a houseful in a minute.
A lad in a sweatshirt comes up with the flowers,
white chrysanths in the shape of a heart,
and I sign the card 'Sister Ruth, Bill and Family'.

Auntie Olive. My auntie Olive, though I don't
give her a thought. Or Donald, though we don't know
what he'll do now. I'm busy thinking
how I'll look in Dad's jacket and those brogues.
They're all coming, from as far as Long Eaton

and Stoke. Our Joss is back with the milk.
He's remembered the matches, and we light up,
a last cup, with a drop of brandy. I stand
to tie and retie the smart new tie in the mirror.
Dad's jacket's alright, but his shoes are like boats.

Living Room

The window is a blue
square dulled by net curtains.
The carpet strange beneath my bare feet.
Upstairs the bath is filling. In my hand

a cake of soap and the towel I forgot.
In my head an engagement ring. The clock ticks.
I stop my heart my body stutters –
a murmur – and at once it passes

but I sit down from respect. Odd
sitting naked in an armchair. In its own time
the water rises, and I know she was right.
I picture bubbles at the lip of the enamel, before

it pours over, becoming clearer, clear,
glazing the blue patch of lino.
Already cool, it slides under the door,
eventually to the stairs, down a step,

three steps at a time. The house,
the town, my head is empty. It's over.
I stand, take a breath,
and go up for my bath.

5th September 1989, Small Hours

Do you exist here, where
the cat like a dancer treads among glasses
upturned for tomorrow and then on to
the table open-leaf and clothed
against an unfamiliar wall
ready for the buffet? Are you
in the chair you occupied for under a year
but almost continually the short days
in this more practical flat? Days
you spoke your mind as never before,
preferring till then to let Mother
speak for the both of you, but gradually
making up for it with all those vanished
friends and enemies, until it became
yammering, yap-yapping, Abide With Me.
Lucid moments came less and less
to break our hearts. They came for you.
You sat in that chair, resisted,
looked up, said clearly, 'Should you go, Tony?'
When he nodded, you said 'Alright.' It was
everything I'd heard, that place.
I couldn't believe it, the curled rocking shells
in the day-room like to like,
the others to and fro in the corridor, needing
money, the way to a bus, who couldn't fathom
the cunning handles on the doors.
I can't believe we put people
in that place together. You're in a better place?
I can't believe that either.
But you're not here, and won't be,
not in my lifetime at least. Now the cat
is in among the bottles, brandy, rum,
whisky, port, sherry – Mother says
they intend washing you over Jordan,
that you never learned to swim. One bottle
staggers and falls, but doesn't break.
The cat peers down at it, very still,
as if willing it to move.

Language

She wasn't going to have the knife
and she didn't, tablets putting her right,

which was noat but an ulcer, thank the Lord.
God's good and the Devil's not a bad'un,

we've not starved a winter yet, and now in this smaller flat,
central heating, cheaper rent, there's less of

Come by this fire, I'm cold, and
Get something to eat, I'm hungry.

But still, Wednesdays was a walk round the table, and
Do like they do in Sheffield: do wi'ert.

Never much bothered, and less bothered these days
though switching the telly off at bloody bleedin blindin swearing:

'I don't friggin swear.' When Joss came in it was
A top-coat warmer out there, and Half-pint won the Tote.

If you couldn't believe it, you
Looked at him gone-out.

Daft as a brush, that was him and that was Dad,
and Police Squad was too daft to laugh at.

I was the scholar, though even reading a map it was
You want to save your eyes, you're bloody studying again.

He was a clever man, my dad, though I didn't notice
and no one said. He was a daft bat, a crazy mare,

who left school at twelve, they all did. Not much
to say, and what they said was Tek no notice,

I've come to that conclusion.
But they wouldn't swap me, not for all the tea in China,

though I'll never have no money
so long as I've a hole in my arse.

stares. That's how you know it's a wolf
and not a dog, George says. Someone muddies
the water by introducing the Latin name
Vulpus canis, and we get down to intensive
writing with the matter still in the air.
Because this is poetry, the fox is not red
but a pungent ginger; the tail fizzes out
and the bib it wears and its four white paws
are grey, like rain. It's on a plinth labelled 'Fox'
in Letraset. When Clare prods it in the belly
Linda keeps expecting it to snap at her hand
but then can't resist fiddling herself with the tail
to see if it's really plaster of Paris and wire. It is
getting on for nine. Now we are silent except
for our pens and the teacher's intense questions.
Above us, the air-conditioning whirrs
like drizzle on ferns beside a falling-dark pine-forest.
My girlfriend enters in one of the lines but I know
she'll want out in the next draft. Rain. Rain! What a relief,
the dust was everywhere, in our eyes and up our noses
and choking the many farm and woodland creatures
raised by our writing. And the local harriers too
are very glad of it, with over five miles to go.
And yet, if there ever was a fox
in this undergrowth, it's long since gone, there's only
this one, this one here, but we persevere because
in a moment we can all go for a drink. Then it occurs to me
the fox's snout fits over its jaw like the lid
on a shoebox. And that's it, I push the pad aside
like a cleared dinner plate, and slide back in my chair.
If this is not a poem, I think, reading over my scrawl,
I'd like to know what is.

Agony

As a teenager I plucked
my eyebrows excessively and they are now
24, married, with a small, sensitive skin,
which is very sparse. Is it too late
to start training? It has deepened from petting
to brunette and is very greasy. Frankly
I have almost never slept with a man
and wine has little or no effect
upon my extremely prominent lower jaw.
I wonder is it perverted or just unusual?
You see I feel I'm secretary to a boss who is
frequently away spoiling my youngsters
with sweets and TV. This is an orthodontic
problem isn't it, because it's never for myself,
only for my body. And heaven knows
I don't want to act 'the jealous wife' but he
enjoys making love to me while I'm asleep
and I am getting seriously
continued on page 150 and yet I
never wake up sometimes two and three
bottles in an evening and during these rows
things come out that are best left unsaid,
terrible things about split ends
and the usual creams. Can you help me?

Borrowdale Morning

for Richard

The sun is flat white. A gull labours
through the valley and the valley
recedes like an echo.
Beyond the dew-wet tent-flap
the campsite simmers in mist, and we
lie looking out with our tin bowls of muesli,
a little kettle rattling to the boil.
Then rolling a roll-up for afters. Boots
close-focus in the doorway gasp for dubbin
though what we see's a slice of fells and trees,
new colours we walked in yesterday,
the day before. But this snapshot
is last day and even the youth group are packing up,
pratting about with ridge-poles and Karrimats.
Even the girl next door who sneezes in German
is packing up.

Now we have shadows. A second gull
trails swallow-flight intake walls
and we set-to too, folding: folding
ridge-walks in rain in the brightest
of bright orange cagoules,
folding the wood-smoke pub,
and the walk back stopping to stargaze pee
in the black lane surprised
by a sheep. Folding the hours
of Explorer maps
that fold like a trick
we've not yet mastered

onto our backs

a last staggering look
and we leave all this suddenly by bus then train.

January

1

You stand at the door (you sometimes are
the door) and, according to tradition, look
to the past year as well as to the new;
but me, I'm all for that watch, moving on
in a room so quiet I can almost see
the second finger as it beats against each mark,
though for a while I can't place it, there
by the blank diary on the uncluttered desk.
Mid-morning the beginning of 1993.
We've been to the coast, as we do.
The garlands are down, the tree undressed
and hoovered under, bin-bagged and put out.

2

According to tradition and by name
you look to the past as you look forward, and what is
is people skating on their arses down Slant Gate,
burst pipes, a broken tanker spilling oil,
or the fox's single line of prints
to scramble our ice-locked gate for scraps
we first of all put out for the birds.
Now we put out rind, bread, apples at night,
for him, always the same young fox.

3

Reading by candlelight, next door's telly
on with this year's honours, I saw you,
at that moment, or thought I did, on a long slow track
out of evergreeen woods, the start
of a ridge walk between two counties
when the valley was a stopped snowstorm
and the mountain air was white in our lungs
all morning gradually higher and higher,
my friend and I, what great friends we were then.

Till, reaching a summit, we could look down
with all of nature in our English pocket,
and point out screes and gullies, scattered homes,
and name the named mountains round us
before picking our way back to the pinched-grey lake,
the straggling winter village, the mini-mart and café.
I saw you all right, but your back was turned.

4

Young and old, you give voice to a bell
telling midnight across an estuary,
crossed, uncrossable, the air thick with salt;
and that voice has the gawky confidence
of sharp bright metal; but that voice too
is the round, sober parish bell, the copper tang
of licking an old penny. Its chimes roll by
to where you are; and, at the last of them,
you are here, unassuming, a fox
in that fable of the old fox in his cave,
pretending to be ill and inviting
all the animals to visit him
so he could eat them without having to go out.

Lake

If I didn't look up the water
went on forever, like one of those lakes we heard so much of
from that teacher

from Ontario.
You pulled back smartly and my book obedient to physics lifted,
pulling me back. The row

-locks groaned
and splintered and there was a rising inch of water but it was
safe enough and hot enough

if not, and in
any case soon behind the island we'd break the rule
and swim from the boat.

It was something
to be held by ripples through an afternoon whose two-hour hire
had only just begun.

The novel I read out
made room in the nineteenth century for us though we knew
how the love match must end

because whatever
the obstacles or tracks of possibility those heroines
always got their man.

We took turns
but you loved rowing, being in control; and I liked
being passenger

on that cool,
upswelling water – the vivid drops giving from the tip
of the oar, the

hollow splash
as you struck, pulling us on; until, far enough out
and though the sun

had drifted behind cloud
I put the book down, the struggle from shorts and T-shirts almost
capsizing us as

we abandoned ship.

At Blea Tarn

The water goes nervously off
as you paddle in the shallows.
It's mild for February but even so
and this fell two miles from Grasmere
is public. It's mid-morning.
You're not drunk. We've not just
pedalled out of rime-cast bivvy-bags
and put a blue windchoked flame
under a tiny kettle. We have strolled here
from a youth hostel. You're not sixteen,
there are no girls to impress. You're shivering,
white, determined. How to explain
your nakedness under this grey sky, numb
up to your knees in that clear, black water?

I remember two or three summers
how we'd swim from a hired boat on Grasmere;
and at the end of a high-walled orchard
how you'd strip to sunbathe,
and once read your book like that
through a storm under the dripping trees.
But this is something else. I feel my heart
clench as you stride now, splashing deeper in
until you're swimming.

A Stone in a Drystone Wall

I've lived so long in this wall
I might have been born here. My family
sit round me, hold me in hold me up,
fallen once, built back.
At night the cold and often the rain.
I can feel it, it's not pure.
Part of me's gone, worn away
for the sake of a boundary, for the sake
of keeping one man's sheep
from another man's grass – little more
than scrubland that after all
would be stronger for cropping.

It's still night. I'm aware of the stars
as I am of the seasons, though only for a moment
over the line of forest from my crammed-in angle
do I ever see a star. I can't imagine
which constellation it belongs to.
It is dimmed and flickers
but never quite disappears.
Mostly I remember a time there was daylight,
the sun coming up like a promise honoured,
and being warmed by it.

A Walk

The valley is a train in the distance,
where we walk because if you stay in
you feel bad. Nothing had prepared me
and everything spools back into itself –
a friend has rung about his marriage, so obvious
I can't believe I didn't see it, or say anything,
and we let the matter drop.

We go down the shifting track to the canal
that's stopped at the choked-up lock
and though we cast bread toward the reeds
the mallard we know are there stay put.
The time of year perhaps, walking further, throwing
more bread, they have eggs or young maybe,
we'll have to buy a book on it.

What the Eye Doesn't See

The stationary train that pulls out of the station.
A harbour and island getting underway
across an estuary and out to open sea.
A church moving, as you walk, on the horizon.
The ceiling turning round a single, drunken
lightbulb; or from a spin in an office chair
watching the room like a rubber band unwind
to bring the world back to where you were.

A face smiling as you smile only to be kind.
Copying a yawn, a limp, a twitch or gesture.
Stagecoach wheels turning backwards out of sight.
The flickerbook's lion eating its tamer.
Wind through young wheat making a river,
and who it was forded that water tonight.

A Dream Mistaking a Person for
What He Has Come to Represent

When Ted Hughes stayed at our house
he fried himself a full English breakfast
in a pan the size of a dustbin lid.
The pan had a case like a guitar, and a strap
to strap it to his back like a busker.
But at that moment it was sizzling and roaring.
As was he, a strenuous chef, and too big
if truth be told for our galley kitchen.

We were too shy to ask if any of those
sausages, bacon, eggs, mushrooms, fried bread and tomatoes
were for us. We are not vegetarian
and we were hungry and the larder and fridge
now empty. *It is a wise man*, he said at last,
settling himself at our breakfast bar
and making free with the brown sauce,
who owns his own frying pan.

Aldeburgh

We turn our backs on the green glow at Sizewell
and trudge along the pebble beach, the waves
steady despite the breeze that chivvies us. New moon
at our elbow and the sky an upside-down bowl of stars.
We've set off from the guest house the wrong way
and don't know we'll miss the party and won't care.
Nearer, black shapes are anglers behind huge umbrellas –
one stands to cast and we change our path, then another
clambers from the sea inside his own travelling glow,
like Dante before we work it out (a halogen lamp).
In a meteor storm it occurs to me we could make
any number of wishes, and when you look up
at the moon and motionless stars, I see you
here, now, as if really for the first time.
You're my wife, but that's not why I love you.

Bliss

Only laziness held him back. He could do
anything, when in that instant it seemed
there was no time. In the tin-hut Sunday School
he'd learned three score and ten, like all of us,
but he was short-changed by tachycardia.
Beneath him the green rich-watered lawn,
the tattered tree, the frangipani's dropped, still-
dropping single sweet flower by his as yet
undiscovered death; all of it brighter than real,
and seen from above like a film or a scene
remembered from the novel. Thirty feet up,
weightless, he stopped, not floating, just being there;
and though he always laughed at the idea
of an afterlife, 'Waiting for admittance' came to him,
a line in a song he didn't know he knew.
He looked round, it might be the last time
and, though the bifocals lay beside his book and body,
he saw easily the new estate: house after house
at which Jimbo and that dog of his delivered
the late paper; and there was Mrs Deidre
hacking at her columbine; and there was Peter;
but mostly he saw their own verandah
where his friends and wife were not panicked
or thinking differently about him, and no one
had rung for an ambulance. From this angle
how clearly he could read their shapes,
a language that was new to him, the chiming
just-touched wineglasses, the loose neckline
of his wife's blouse and how it was
he'd come to marry her. It was very like music,
in fact it was in a way a kind of music
that filled his head, what he could see of everyone,
what he could remember and understand,
until night rung by rung decants last moments
into a blue earthenware jug, into brimming glasses,
a lifetime, into their hands, into his.

At the End of Here

It's quite right to imagine them as they cluster
shivering on the near bank, waiting for the ferry.
Already they're not people but exhibits.
They're saying their lost causes, their successes,
and it's a museum, this sloping shingle beach
out of season, without visitors, except themselves,
and unaware of each other – which is just as well
because they're all pitifully naked
next to the funfair, the boarded-up arcade,
the crescent of hotels still with winter lettings,
air-conditioning and a sea view to every room,
like the one we look out from. It's no longer night,
and now, as a liner appears on the horizon
it's warmer and filling slowly with colour.
You can see them quite clearly, though distant,
despite the sea fret. You can see their faces.
Do you recognise any? Take a good look –
it's not easy I know, not least because,
though they got up from their graves to be here,
though they unburned and remade themselves to wait
for a short journey by water, across a river
whose name if asked is on the tip of their tongue,
you notice they're none of them as they were,
you notice they're all of an age,
in their prime, in their twenties,
even the senile, even the cot-death,
and as it were with all their lives before them.

Whitby

1

I woke in the middle of my days
still wearing those off-white cords
and with a three-day beard and a tune
in my head from a party I left early.
I look at my hands and see what's been done
with them, all the things they had to carry.
It'll be different now, I think, finding
a kettle and a toaster and opening a tin
for the cat that seems to live here.
Salt in the air tells me it's the coast.

Which is how I come to sit in this high room,
though I could go higher, and look out
on three sides round at town, sea and harbour,
and I know that nothing is accounted for;
and it's like looking back looking out
from these two rented storeys, and seems to say
that everything delights in change, though we know
with change what must follow, in just the way
the wake of a herring boat breaks
and is spent still in mid-channel.

2

Down there, the harbour is oil, in which
spilt lights are broken and healed over, broken:
houselights and two hundred steps up
the floodlit church laid out in a yellow splodge.
Walk further, through the stale smell of fresh fish
where tied-up herring boats are slack
in the water: coils of rope, diesel, grease;
and the green stern light one brilliant splash.

3

Stillest at night and, except the air
is thick with salt, it might simply be a river.
It is, even though the moon above it
fails to light the landscape it feeds
black as far as the eye can see, and beyond,
where everything that moves delights in change,
slow lights moving left to right, north to south,
trawler, ferry, or another boat coming home,

which at length, dawdling, is let run
with the tide, then brought round at the quay
by a bubbling throttle. Dead-calm, sloppy,
this water is to the sea beyond the bar
like dusk-heightened streetlights are
to the same lights at midnight, each route
and dwelling in the town replaced by distance
which the night has made a collar of jewels.

Sitcom

The baby is at an age to say Oh fuck,
the middle one sleeps off E with her boyfriend
and has her prints taken shoplifting.
The eldest has his arse in the sofa
and trails a guitar lead even to the loo;
Oasis make him sneer at exams.
The gas electric mortgage council tax road tax
and catalogue in the same week is a joke,
not to mention the phone, tied up twenty-four hours
with trauma to step over on the stairs.
The cats bring fleas and a coating of fur.
The job is runnning to stand still and everyone else
in a company car or sleeping rough.
Your dad died convinced you were his dad.
Mum is trapped by her legs in a flat
you don't visit enough. And your friends –
your friends are a box of bastards you never see.
You love your wife and your wife loves you
but neither of you believe it.

Some night by chance

Some night by chance you'll meet a man
who says your thoughts – a band a book a film,
parents. He'll drink the same drink and smoke your brand,
guess the punchline and still laugh. You won't kiss
or hold hands even for days of meeting
accidentally on purpose. Can you believe this?
His eyes stop your heart. You grin like idiots.

Some night by chance you'll meet a man
on the last bus. He asks directions
to some other place but then gets off after you.
There are streetlights but you're nervous, his step
a moment behind yours, which quickens, not quick
enough by the blade of dark, the garages
he pushes you towards. Is this more likely?

Or else one night you meet a man in Sainsbury's say.
He's married or living with, you can see that
from the trolley, and yet there's something there
when you catch his eye on cereals, sauces, the jam aisle.
You pay at adjacent checkouts. Go
as if agreed into the café, the only free table.
And he is both those other men. Believe me.

Clinical Depression

I drove that way thirty virtuous miles
with the dozen years of our growing up,
to say I'm here and sit with him in the dayroom
once a week for a month, though he was there
longer. Brother. Half brother.
Film star cheekbones from Dad's side
and the thin mouth, wet eyes. One day
we walked by the res across the road. Sailing boats
need rowing boats or dinghies; at anchor
the breeze nods their masts. Boys went by
on mountain bikes and we talked and got nowhere,
in the end back to the block he suddenly
can't believe is right. He knows I get things wrong,
so has to see my car in the carpark, go round
and see the key fit the lock before he'll try
the automatic doors, the corridors, and still
there's a panic not to be wrong, to read
the curious ward name and know he's home.
Which is when I'm stopped by the ECT
he signed himself to. What do I know?
His sister thought it would work, they had to
try something. And as she pointed out later,
'cheaper than drugs, cheaper than talk'
that's just politics, and this is not about me,
and his wife, whatever you say, every night,
every morning, will stay dead.

Death Cap

When the phone goes at half past one
I'm already dressing in my head, already getting
in the car, whose floored accelerator wakes
the whole street. But it's your friend

who just thought she'd ring
with the name of that mushroom
that was on the tip of your tongues all day.
She knew we'd want to know. And so

the old woman sprawled between the loo
and fallen walking frame, the teenager
with a wrist open to some despair, and the brother
who looked stupidly the wrong way and stepped

in front of what threw him in the air –
these, and the mugging, the rape,
the boy who choked to death on a boiled sweet,
they all belong to others, elsewhere. And so,

being up, and with nothing tomorrow
to be up for, we put the kettle on,
like people do when there's nothing to be done.

And so God bless you Pauline Bellamy,
you and your killer mushroom –
we raise our cups to you.

Summer Evening

after Stanley Cook and for Lesley Jeffries

Every summer comes an opaque evening
before the beach is photos and the leaves
let go to relight autumn. It's brisk in Wickes
and the garden centre's scented colours
are loaded in the backs of estates. In parks
that saw offices undress for lunch
lads career in the wake of the World Cup
and wood after deliberate wood finds
a path in its own curve to the jack.
Everywhere is couples, and pushchairs
that make sense of last year or last but one,
till pubs overflow round continental tables
on main roads, laughing like it might last.

Sooner or later, swans on a river
disprove the moon they paddle through,
cameoed by willows. The rowing boat
moored there is a temptation you decline,
though all the time you walk, taking
the long cut through the park, you imagine
being out on that water, the drag
and viscous ripples as you pull,
then shipping the oars and just letting it drift.

Baker Street: Poet in Residence (Day 1)

My bag not holding a bomb, it's ticketed
with St Michael, and I queue for a pass
among expense accounts, chic that fits in
in London, or this part. I'm from the sticks
and the receptionist's never heard of me.

The marble foyer is stately home,
but a swirl of steps leads straight to the end
of the twentieth century, a corridor of offices
and Fairtrade tea, 'Hello, hello, so pleased';
before I'm kidgloved round the works:

rooms big-windowed like a zoo to meet
IT, this designer, that, CAD
in a cube of dummies up close with real
needle and thread, this neck of the woods
like a liberal college, all colour and coffee-cups.

The smoking room when I get there's
a meritocracy of horses for courses,
sweatshirt and Armani. A woman like a model,
who is a model, exact size 10 for a living,
nods at my notebook, 'That your camera?' then

a brilliant hill of bananas wheeled by from nowhere.
Next's an airlock you need a smart card for
against industrial espionage. It seems to be
labels for soup tins. Further, Furniture,
and not knowing where to look through Lingerie.

More smiles. Finally shake hands with Press
and on the way back in a crossroads of plush
and softlighting a director with the air
of a man in a light-up bowtie: 'Not typical,' Julia says,
'but then none of them are.' As an afterthought

pop in here, wall-to-wall front-loaders putting jumpers
in eight hours through five years of hot cycles.
What it is to be lambswool, shrunk hardly at all
at the end of the day but bobbled enough to call
the entire line back from Paris, Hong Kong, Dublin, Strasbourg,

Huddersfield.

To Autumn

You come breezing in. It's all yours for a while,
make yourself at home. A leaf detaches itself
from how we look at it, dates are underlined
in still-to-be-backed books, and wasps
that helicoptered by dustbins are brown now

and taxi on the kitchen floor, their stings
the most alive thing about them. Danger, my dear,
come away. There are ash keys to spin for you
and conkers to swing, wide-eyed fireworks,
and Santa to believe in already in the shops.

Words for Paul Cézanne

The town museum banned me from its walls
till there wasn't a canvas it could afford.
By then I was twenty years dead, of course.
Not that I wanted for money or for the fame
that came late to drive me from my home.
My friend Zola had his bestsellers and throve;
Renoir, whose one commission could buy
and sell me a thousand times, bought me.
I copied Chardin, Corbet; their fruit was flesh
just as it is, as if it might rot in the paint.
Mine was art. Don't look to me for life,
only oils and a palette knife. They say I walked
into town with my paintings on my back
like a Christ. A little joke. I smiled,
and knew my work, and set to work.
I loved my son. My wife was dutiful.
After, she said I'd no idea. I loved the landscape
that grew out of me, and you see how it was.
Not master of myself then, or even in this,
I am a man who did not, does not exist.

Top Withens

Moors that on this good walking day are empty
far as the horizon, the cloud they merge in. Up here
three daughters are set loose to be themselves
and more than that, peopled by characters, tiny seeds
of a disease that flourished, biding its short time.
Their mother dead, their father had God to answer to,
and answered. What we know of them is books,
the youngest on a blue velveteen sofa in a cold room
admitting the doctor only in terror hours before she died.
The middle girl also vanished. It was the eldest
who married success and wandered here ten years
bundled in words that broke her heart, recalling them
and the brother they made not-famous. What we know,
that beguiling warmth of reconstruction,
can't keep out the chill that killed her and her child,
however it is we say out loud her living name.

You'll Like This

Word of mouth from dinner packs the evening out,
and what he learned then he puts in now,
names mainly for butts of jokes and flattery
like clairvoyance. Best is completely at random
to bring the local hardman up on stage,
blind in the lights, polite. And to lift a tenner,
and to open his mouth by turning an ear
for an egg to pop out and calling him duck.
Pit villages, he has all the patter, near the knuckle
on inbreeding and the little lad lost in the woods,
but he's a highwire act and risk is part of the trick.
Committee men's nicknames put him good
and 'Society Row' at Edlington.
It's a night out alright and they split their sides
while he's straightfaced through the wreckage,
a little man still rough round the edges,
wide-eyed, brilliant, desperate, two years from telly …
When the hardman twigs and goes to go for him
but can't get off the stool. The air's blue
with what he'll do to him and this lot, all of them
crying with laughing, till a click of the fingers
releases him, blind in the lights, the last half hour blank
and the conviction that that onion's a Granny Smith.
Finally, hands him grandly from thin air a tenner
for being a sport, with the understanding
he'll stand some of these many good friends a drink.

Beard

At twenty, needing to look older
than fourteen, I grew one that lived with me
ten years. Clipped trim, and with that hair –
though I didn't admire him – people said
'Noel Edmonds'. 'Well, if I had his millions.'
Still expecting I would. Not that full-face black,
mountaineer or deputy head, looking down
from the clouds. Nor that raggedy don't-mind-me
on men who, even built like prop-forwards, manage
to look small. I know, I know lovely, brighter, wiser men
who carry them off, even a goatee, even sideburns,
and wasn't it Thatcher who wouldn't have a beard
in the cabinet? Two sides to every stereotype.
But mine was a boy's and my wife finally told me
to grow up. I thought of this nicking the tip
of my nose with a fixed head disposable.
There's time to grow a beard, Dad said,
when you're six foot under. He was wrong,
and they'll burn me too, and what I remember
is the stuck-on bits of loo roll that gave way
in the end to silvery stubble
like a hermit or a sage, the mask he wore
when nothing made sense, alone there
in that place among so many of his kind.

About Time

A ticking box, each and every one identical
as flakes that touch a roof to win a bet,
and as unique. Count them down with Big Ben
before you turn to kiss a stranger, let in luck
with a slice of bread, a piece of coal, 10p.
Look back on moments as many, different
and the same, as people on the homeless streets.
Two thousand years and the church as full tonight
as a supermarket or *Songs of Praise*. The flakes
that fall and drift make most of anonymous,
and though it's true that through them we can see
the changes (medicine say) that no one would disown,
what matters, it comes to me at last, is that that stranger
through the trackless snow has your name, mine.

Teeth

The pain stops just being here, tipped back
like a space shot. One look and
'You don't like dentists,' he says. Fluent in gargle,
he understands my 'Never met one'
is a joke that's true. Young, Asian, expert,
he arrived from the other end of a mobile number
on a Sunday in a black new Porsche
to calm me and put a bit of the wrong right.

A night and a morning kneeling by a sink
running cold across it brought me to this
partitioned room, the leather hydraulic chair,
besting thirty years of shame as much as fear
and complacency, a weakness in character
that keeps my smile closed and lifts my hand
to a surprised laugh. And it's class and laziness too,
that gap between what's learned and what

you're born with. I submit to his white coat
and instruments, look up into a sci-fi sun,
while all the while my wife holds my childish hand
just this side of fainting. It's over in minutes
and I can rinse and get to my feet white-faced
in a drug-company mirror. 'There's more to be done'
(a man of understatement), and she takes his card
in case I change my mind and who I am and want to be,

from a family with a grinning glass by the bed,
only wearing them for best, their faces wrong,
and slipping them into a hanky to eat.
What's left of mine's mine, and the damage too,
I know that. Like my talk, not one or the other,
theirs or ours, in a world still us and them.
One thing's sure: I'll come back. I'll come back
when it hurts enough.

My Mother on a Seat Outside a Hospital

Too early for the bus, Mum and Aunt Tad
have walked a dozen dark-to-daylight miles
through a wood, by quiet roads,
to sit on a bench beside a flower bed, colours
that release their scent in the evening,
and wait while her husband dies on a ward
already awake, that she might have visited after all.

He was the man before my father,
young, clean-shaven, just moved where work was.
If he'd not loved swimming, or had known
that pool, which end was which,
or had simply shallow-dived, I'd not exist;
and Mum too would be a different person.
She never told me this, someone else did,

how she lost the love of her life, a young wife
with two babies – my big sisters – and with my brother
forming inside her, who must manage now
alone in a strange town between the wars.
But there she is, just as she is, so I can see
through that depth of water the spine
snapping, and the man who was not my father

bobbing to the air ... It took him days to die
there, where, outside on a municipal bench,
two young women, girls they call themselves,
are anxious and not tired, deciding – despite
the sixth sense that brought them there –
from kindness to give it another half hour
before bothering anyone so early.

Crich Stand

A tiny light in all that sea, gone five seconds
and twenty-seven years. One hot July
past chucking-out time, we stepped not very drunk
from the Duke of Sussex, six of us, and saw
the landlocked lighthouse. Twenty miles. And set off
there and then to walk all night the White Peak
ups and downs of chevronned lanes; the sky
so very close, so many stars and wishes,
names of constellations over charcoal wheat,
and fingerposts, galleon trees, unseen cattle
lumbering, then a fox that looked through us
and strolled on. In time we stopped, six of us,
somewhere in Derbyshire, where the tower swung
exploding eye-to-eye across the drystone fields.
At seventeen, who needs Dr Freud to say
what it was; and as it is we stood in its wash,
blinded; then turned without a word, our shadows
thrown before us, dreams breaking in
even as we walked, heads down, the half hour
to a bus home. I thought of this today
on what's left of the coast in that neck of the woods,
our old stamping ground, the last place on earth.

and we walked up to school although we knew the school
was closed, a day of sledging on baking trays,
and Spike the Snowman with his dog, Snowy.
The butcher crunched with us the short cut
late and later for work through the little park
and got trapped by his childhood –
rolling the torso, weightlifting the head between us,
and sculpting, setting berries into eyes,
a twig instead of a carrot and bigger twigs for arms.
Our hands burned. All the while the shaken flakes fell
closing the world to the dome of the park
far as the eye and the mind's eye could see.

Ted Savoury

Mr Savoury Duck, who arrived in an ambulance
he converted himself, delivering a music hall
every Tuesday without fail till lumbago
and supermarkets retired him at eighty.
Teabags and tins were no dearer than town, and rabbits
were fanfared alive by the ears, or strung up
for Mum to skin with a razor blade for Christmas.
My first football boots really were boots
with the studs nailed in; and his out-of-date
jams and pickles stopped just short of deadly,
though his real talent was getting the world to see
it needed a new mangle or antler coat-stand,
then turning up next week with the very thing.
He stepped out of Dickens before I could read,
with a yard of geese and half a dozen porkers,
and a house up to the rafters in stuffed bears
and cuckoo clocks, unless they were a story
to match the whiskers he grew, a stage-prop,
like the waistcoat and bowtie and cherrywood pipe.
I was eight when he brought the sit-up-and-beg,
huge cast-iron I'd dismount proud at first then
second nature by running it into our hedge,
a feat that from this distance sums up those days
of after the war and before give peace a chance.
And if he earned an honest living by cheating,
everyone knew the rules he didn't play by,
and bought from his van not in spite of but because.

Breakfast in the Dunblane Hilton

When you were young you said you'd rather die than live to be old.
And yes, perhaps you would rather.

Dorothy Nimmo

I read, surprised by your self, some of your poems –
wise, clear-eyed, cantankerous –, and find
among the Earl Grey, the Frank Cooper's Vintage Oxford,
that I'm crying. Which isn't what your words meant
or even your death. Reading, I'm with you,
not here, this white cloth, electric candelabra,
the Highlands glazed and cut off in frames; until
the big windows green with spring are opened
and the breeze brings a playground's happy chaos
to where we sit. And then, when their bell goes, I remember
just where I am. And close the book, though not
your voice, which stays open – here, like anywhere
you chose to look and listen, and to speak
your mind, your surprised, surprising heart.

Anyone for Tennis?

For its own sake, not for a team or any ambition;
though getting better was everything just then,
at the limit of a junior season ticket
for the gravel courts of Sutton Lawn, with its
leaning pavillion and pissy changing room,
the misspelt grafitti and pulled-out sinks proof.
Mam bought us whites and later matching caps
delighted to find just the thing in Skegness,
and we must have looked prats. Still, our first serves
went in, the topspin backhands put on weight,
and every smash and drop-shot was two fingers
to exams around the corner, that long wet summer.
And when it rained we played on, the meteor
of sopping green splat a passing shot
that left me splay footed, unsighted as I was
by the girl next door flailing for a lob
bra-less in her soaked-through shirt. Advantage us,
me and my best mate, but with no more idea
than chalk dust raised by ace after towering ace
at the All England Club, Wimbledon.

Ironing

The perfect release of a limited aim.
Stanley Cook

I like it best when there's time to see myself
through the drizzle of a weekday morning,
with Woman's Hour or a talking-book detective,
and forsythia defining the universe
beyond the propped but empty line. I like
deckchairing the board and plugging in,
the glug of filling the chamber. Then to set off
on the floral reflective cover, a time
that's its own purpose, all faults and craters
levelled to the end of the week. And nothing else
till it's done. Nosing through steam round a button,
powering up the straights of T-shirts,
down the Forth Bridge of a kingsize quilt,
the worst that can happen a cascade of pleats
or a stain to put back soaked in Vanish.
Yes, I've scorched my thumb and melted the nap
from favourite velvet. Yes, that was me, too,
the iron print on the lino. But no,
that was only a joke, the cauliflower ear
of ironing when somebody rings up. And look,
there's the kitten bedded down like an advert in it
with her fleas. The world won't look at me
and say how I've let myself go, the world that loves
to wrinkle and crease and say I told you so.

Sheffield by Night

After the nightclubs have turned out and before
the cleaners have plugged in, the city is as still
as a snowglobe this last day of summer.
I sweat up Paradise St that was Workhouse Rd
and out under green-lit trees of the cathedral
like strolling through an artist's impression;
then over new tramtracks that dad would know
as far as the Cutler's Hall and HSBC.
A dog walking itself in the corner of my eye
past Pollards is gone before I see it's a fox.
Next, Boots the Chemists bright as a cruise ship
but the *Marie Celeste*; then over Fargate
and down Chapel Walk, the Link, the Samaritans,
and double-take at shoes a month's wages;
past the delivery-end of M&S now turn left
by the Crucible. I'm not mugged
in the subway or offered sex to feed a habit.
Ghost roadworks on the steep bit of Flat Street
and in the waking Interchange Paul Simon's
got that ticket still for his destination.
The Grade II listed eyesore on the skyline
is a memory of the Socialist Republic
and in its people-centred daring typical
of Sheaf Field, home of the cyclepath and bendi
-bus, the most wooded city in Europe if you
don't listen to Brum, and the most parks too,
that turned the steelworks into a shopping centre,
and the shopping centre into another world –
then suddenly here, at what I think of as Midland Station,
to carry this lightheaded flu to Nottingham.

On Not Being George W. Bush

The ice-cream carpet, that was one of mine.
And powdered water, wine-gum wine,
jelly windows, see-through cats;
and yo-yo cornflakes, interstellar bobble-hats –
all mine. And mud television and underwater sky,
not to mention the *Who What Why*
Book of Bread. But the river of the recent dead,
that was some other guy.

L.O.V.E.

I live in your heart, biding my time.
Talk with me in a rhyme
or waiting-room paperback.
I bring out the Barry Manilow in you.
The reddest rose appears in your life
and with it the desert pillow.
I am blind, which may be why
I walk you into doors,
metaphorically, literally,
always the last to know.

I'd heard about the man, who, drunk

I'd heard about the man who, drunk, stood up
and said, This is where I get off, then opened
a moving door and jumped. A friend
of a friend pulled the communication cord.
It came to mind and I told the story, and then
this person remembered standing next
to a boy who lowered the window,
and stuck out his head. Decapitated,
was all she said. But I saw a guillotine
and the torso turning back, going on
like they say a chicken does, and this person
stepping aside to let the boy go
wherever it was he last thought he should go.
And so when this person said Are you really
married, it was easy to say Oh yes.

On the Road

I'd like to be a lorry driver, sometimes,
if it weren't for reversing, manoeuvring
in towns, if it weren't for unloading
and customs. My reward
the greasy joes, a jukebox like Brian Matthews,
a game of pool, and a calendar of girls
in the cab, their smile in October and November
the most they wear. I'd like sometimes
to drive a lorry A-known to B-known
and the route between to a deadline
with a stop-over in a lay-by and the kettle
plugged in the cigar lighter.
And to smoke again incidentally
Player's No. 6 like everybody,
nearside lane a steady 65,
wipers this year next year this,
the continent an adventure,
the moon over pine forest, if it weren't
for the ring-road, the tachometer,
if it weren't for the belly
and the beard our Johnno shaved off
they said (it was a talking point) before
he hung himself that morning
in a warehouse outside Crewe,
despite a wife, waiting,
despite a child.

Born-again bikers,

top of the range and all the leathers, at their age,
instead of an affair or throwing up the job,
off they go unwinding miles of moonlight road,
travelling in hope, tip-toeing icy bends,

slipstreaming lorries, and wheeling down
the outside of jams, at their age, ducking the Welsh
speed cameras, clocking the gear in Matlock Bath,

and, well, why not, if they see the danger now
they couldn't afford then
and still ride, still open her up,
letting the years fall behind

good luck to them. Haven't I after all
taken up piano.

The Wife of Bath's Tale
as retold by Gladys Ruth Sansom (eighty-six)
of Sutton-in-Ashfield, Notts.

Never had much time for Charlie, but he's all reight to talk to. Day
he come, fost thing he said was he wor fair clammed. Mrs, he said,
me stomach thinks me throat's cut. I said Well it's bread and
drippin, else you'll have to do like they do in Sheffield. He said
What's that (never been to Sheffield, only to visit). I said, Do
wi'ert. He laughed and said bread and drippin it is then.

Bread and drippin! As if folks'd give royalty bread and drippin! Our
Joss'd oppened a tin of ham. It wor all done ready in kitchen under
a teatowel. He worn't on his own, the Prince, nayther. We had a
houseload, and it's not a big flat, them as look after him and such,
and them for the telly, and they all wanted snap and a cup of tea.

After he'd had a bite, he said, Well Mrs, you know why we're
here. I said Aye I do an'all, but it's not me as you want, you want
Clara Do-Rose. He looked at me gone-out, but you're a widder
three times ovver, and my man here said that you know. I said
That's as may be, but it's Clara Do-Rose as you want. She knows.
She can give you your answer. Well, Clara knows what women
want, and no bogger'd argue with Clara. Mind, I've not seen her
since the war. There was that Yank, Doodle Bug we christened
him on account of his tash, but she stuck by her Malcolm, with his
foot blown off, even though he was neither use nor ornament,
never wanted no bogger looking at his foot, even Clara, even in
the dark. Well it don't figure for me, me duck, she told him, but it
were no good, might as well tek a dolly to bed. Even then give her
her due, she never let Doodle Bug do as he liked more than twice
else three times, and she were drunk as a lord one of them as I
know to, because I were wi' her in a car one of them old uns like
you don't see now. It worn't his, we just saw it parked up, and it
were bitter cold and they didn't lock up in them days so he said,
Let's gerrin here for a warm. I were in front with, now who wor I
wi'? Clara and Doodle Bug wor in back, hardly got started when
door oppens and it's this Captain whose car it wor.

Anyroad. Next item on the agenda it's Clara hersen, he must have had her sent for. Never thought to see her in my house. She'd changed. I said, I'd not know you Clara. And I wouldn't, not with that hair, she had lovely hair. Grow it another couple of inch, you could sit on your hair, that's what her Malcolm said. What would I want to sit on me hair for, she said, me arse'll do me for sitting on. If there's anything wants growing by two inch, Malcolm Dodd, you know where it's billeted. Grow that and I'll sit on it for you. He went bright red, it was in the tap room of the Traveller's, and we were all theer. She didn't care, Clara. I wonder Malcolm didn't land her one, and I think she'd warrant it some nights specially when we'd been out on the qv, but he didn't have the means. Aye, you *do* me lad, you so much as offer, she said, and I'll box your bleedin blindin ears. She had a mouth on her, did Clara, but she had a right hook too. I don't hold with language, not for women anyroad, but she didn't have no choice, he was always so boggering sorry for his-sen, Malcolm.

Anyroad up, the Prince says he'll have another if there's one in the pot and now Clara's here we can get started. Nice manners, but you expect that of royalty. You don't notice his ears so much to his face. But it worn't Clara Do-Rose, not with that hair and her bent double like a safety pin. That worn't the Clara I knew, any bogger could see it worn't her, but I thought if it meks him happy good luck to him, and it did because she says, Yes, she says, I can tell you, and I'm the only one as can.

The prince said, You can? Room went quiet: well, it matters, this, to him. Because his mam's had this message from God in the middle of doing a jigsaw of their house, about handing on the reins or throwing the towel in for good. She said God had said, Let Charles tek ovver now lass, only you've got to set him a test fost. She says What's that then God? He says, There's more women in your country than men, and it's not reight as things stand, women should have more say. So for a start your lad Charles has to tell you what it is that women want. And this answer, what women want, it's got to be an answer that not one woman in the country'd disagree wi'. Either he tells you that or he don't get the kingdom, no bogger does, because it's going to be one of them like France or America where they don't have no royalty. Tell him he's got a year and a day, God says. Then he thinks again and says, Nay, with all this helicopters and satellites and such tell him he's got a week.

So Charles, he goes rushin round like a blue-arsed fly. Asking everybogger. Archbishop of Canterbury, Chief of Police, Lionel Blair. Then he has a brainwave and asks his dad, what he thinks it is his mum wants. Apparently Philip says, I don't know as she wants owt, lad, she's not short of a bob or two. But he's been tipped the wink that Charles has to ask a widder three times ovver living round our way. In a council flat. Course that's me, and here we are. But it worn't me.

And Clara Do-Rose, or her as says she's Clara Do-Rose, says again, Yes, and I'm the only bogger on God's earth as *can* tell you. And it wor reight quiet, as I say, apart from the chuntering of them cameras. Then she says, I'll tell you summat for nowt, though, that sort of information don't come cheap. Now Clara's Malcolm wor like that, so mean he wouldn't let you light a candle off his lamp; but not Clara. She were always oppenhanded. We'd say, Clara you'll never have no money so long as you've a hole in your arse. And bonny, she wor proper bonny, and now I think on she wor a lot like that wife of his what killed hersen or ran off with a foreigner, I know it wor summat o' sort. Car crash that wor it, I think. I do know they took snooker off. Nowt on telly, Joss said, that Princess Dinah's died. Aye, it wor a long day that one.

But this Clara Do-Rose, when she said that about it not coming cheap, well she looked just like one of them what-do-you-call-its. I'm not joking. Manny and mardarse at same time. Charlie says, Mrs, you can name your price.

Door went just then. It wor our Joss, he'd been out for more milk. They'd only got sterra, he says, and, By, it's a top coat warmer out theer. And he stops, cos cameras's going. But this is what they want, the news men. Cameras going and it's all lit up for the telly. I'll mash some tea, he says, and he goes.

She says, I don't want no money. There's this pause. And she says, I want him. And she points at this young feller as is with the prince. Not long out of school, by the looks on it. Not married, are you me duck? she says and he laughs but she's not laughing.

Sorry Mrs, the prince says, Sir Dooins is not for sale, ask for anything, what do you want: wealth, jewellery, a palace ...

She says, I've always fancied owning a race horse. And Charlie's face lights up. But no, she says, only Sir Dooins here will do, his hand in marriage. She grins her one-tooth at him, and gives him this wink. Charlie tells the telly men to turn their tackle off and bogger off out onto the landing.

When they've gone, Sir Dooins says, Mrs, I will marry you whenever you wish. Charlie says, You'll do no such thing Gerald or Jason or whatever his name is. And this lad says, But Your Highness, it's not for my country, I'm doing it for you. I thought he wor going to cry, the prince, he wor that moved. You can hear the clock going now, too big for the room. Charlie sits reight still for a bit like he's thinking reight hard, says summat quiet to the lad, who nods, and then says summat else quiet to the man with the briefcase, and this man says, We'll have one of them contracts drawn up.

Nay, says Clara, we don't need no contracts. If you agree here and now to wed me, no lawyer'll wangle you out on it, not in this world. What do you say? And the lad, this Sir Dooins, says alright and they shake hands, I do this for the Prince. Clara says (and you've got to remember she's seventy, nay she'll be eighty-odd) she says, Give ovver, it's nowt to do with him, you can't help yoursen can you? Men, you're all the same, led ovver the fields by your willy-nilly.

Not fields though, now, it's all built up round that way. Tek the precinct. I remember when it was Idlewells, though I lived out at Bleak Hall in them days, Tod's Row it wor called then. Oh yes, tell you who I went to school wi' as you'll know: Harold Larwood. Pub named for him now up Annesley. It'd surprise if me dad isn't in there this minute, though I can't tell you the last time he called round here. It's a few years. A good few years since I've seen me dad. I don't know where he is these days tell the truth. He said, don't you worry, you can take your hat off, Fanny Ann, I can see you've had your hair cut. He never wanted me to have me hair cut, didn't me dad. Finest fast bowler England ever had and he might just as well have not bothered if you ask anybogger. Harold Larwood. Harold Larwood, George Formby, you don't hear nowt on them nowadays, Dr Steiney, you never see him nayther. Nor our Tony.

So they call back the telly men and set the cameras going for what all women want. Even with all that you can still hear the clock ticking and everybogger holding their breath. Well? the prince says. Hold your hosses, Clara says, you've got to stand up and ask me reight. So the Prince of Wales stands up in my living room and says, Mrs Do-Rose, Tell us now what it is that all women want. And she smiles. You'll notice my fiancé there, he's got lovely big hands, she says, and it's true what they say I can tell you, she says, and that's one of the reasons I decided he wor for me. Women don't want a man for decoration. But nay, I'm only teasing, that's not it, or not all there is to it, not by a long chalk. Anyroad she says, What women want, it's what you'd expect. And she pauses like. Then: Women want to be in charge of their-sens. After a moment Charlie nods, Ay, he says, to be their own boss, like, happen you're right. Me mam'll agree with that I should think. And well, as you know, she does agree an all, and we're into all this parliament rigmarole.

But then it's not a week later, and it's the wedding isn't it in London. I don't go, not with this leg, but I see it on telly like everybogger else. Well Clara's a sight. Old enough to be his grandma and falling down drunk even at the altar, and when it comes to her vows she says I f—in' well do and laughs so you can see she's not reight in head.

All ovver bar the shoutin, I think, when who should come round next day but Charles again, and on his own an all.

Well, we've got nowt in house and it's days since Joss went round with the Ewbank, but he says he's not stoppin. So Joss mashes a pot of tea and finds out a packet of fig biscuits and half a layer of Teatime Assorted. The prince has brought some photos of the happy couple (that's what he called them). Seems as Clara made him bring them for old time's sake. And in the photos it really is Clara Do-Rose. I mean the Clara as was. Beautiful. I couldn't believe it. Charlie pours another cup and tells me how it's come about, which is this: After the wedding, they went somewhere posh for the reception, and after somewhere grand for the wedding night. Well this Sir Dooins, he's a perfect gentleman and even though she's nasty, I mean not just to look at, I mean nasty in hersen, mardy and allus on, like one of them little dogs that pees up your sofa because it can't sink its teeth in your leg. Nevermind that, he's lovely with her all the same. But that's him, Charles says, that's him, generous in his heart, like one of the old-fashioned knights, the knights of the round table, I forget which one he said. It worn't Albert I do know.

And on his wedding night, just as it's dropping dark, he's looking out across at the gardens to the river reight far off, just stood theer, Sir Dooins, at his winder, a bit worried obviously. In comes his bride. He hears but don't turn round at fost. But it's Clara like in the photo, the beautiful Clara Do-Rose, nineteen else twenty. Clara Do-Rose at nineteen. She could pass for nineteen till she wor thirty, as a matter of fact, them nights we went singing down the Market Tavern and the Soldiers and Sailors, the Traveller's Rest, the Dog and Duck, the Staff of Life, touring round. When a song come on the wireless we liked we'd write it down on a sugar bag and practise in front room and go out of a night and sing for us larrup till chucking-out time, pissed up, Malcolm never objected nor mine. So this is Clara as she wor when I knew her. When he turns to her, Sir Dooins can't believe his eyes. This isn't the woman he wed. Ah but it is, she says, I'm Clara Do-Rose reight enough.

And this is it: because you loved me, because you saw into who I wor, this is who I am tonight on our wedding night. Well they hug each other, like they would. Then she steps back. But, she says, you've got to choose. I can be like this, and young as I am now, for only half the time. At night or else in the day. Before or after sunset I have to be the old Clara Do-Rose again. Which is it to be, my husband, she says, old by day or in your bed?

(Joss worn't taking it in at all; he said, They're closing that Kwik-save. Are they really, his Highness says. He's alright, he'll just go down the precinct like he used to. They've finished the precinct, done it up, put a roof on it, made a nice job on it an all.)

Anyroad where wor I? Yes. So Sir Dooins has to choose, day or night. She says, Clara does, You've got till tomorrer to mek your mind up. Quick as a flash, he says, I don't need till tomorrer me duck. I know what my answer is. Clara interrupts, Ayup lad be careful now, I know you men, thrice nightly fost week and it's off down the allotment theerafter – don't you be hasty. Sir Dooins raises his hand. Nay, Mrs, he says, I said I know what my answer is and I'm sticking to it: young by day or young by night, that's for *you* to decide.

Now the prince gets excited telling this and the bottom half of his bourbon's come away in his tea. This is the best part he says, it's like a fairy story, he says because Clara Do-Rose when she hears him say that she's reight glad because now she can be young all the time, and she is. You see, it's like brokken a spell, him saying as it's up to her, seeing as she's her own boss.

I say, So they live happily ever after then do they? Looks like it, he says. And what about you, your highness, I say, you get to be king now do you? He sets off on it but I stop him, I don't need to know all the ins and outs o' Meg's arse. There's the door and it'll be our Maureen and Diane or our Maureen and Mick. But it's me dad. Oh dad, I've fair missed you, I say, I can't think of owt else. And he sits there, large as life, still wi' his boots on. You'll never guess, he says, who I've just been talking wi'. But I know, I don't know how: Harold Larwood, I say, and it wor an all, took the wind out on his sails. But ayup, father, can you see we've got company? Dad, this is the Prince of Wales. Your Highness, this is me dad. And I didn't know where to put me-sen because me dad just said, I can see that, and what's it to me: I only died for such as him. And happen he did because the prince said, Mester, I know as you did, I do know that very well. And they shake hands. By it wor a sight, as if they wor the same man underneath. Well they wor, and that's a thought, your dad and your king as will be, your dad and your king the same man, it struck me all of a sudden. And both on 'em beholden, beholden to me or my kind, and me and my kind beholden to them an all, or to him and his kind, if you follow me, that's how it is. Living or dead, woman or man, then or nar.

Joss

I'm asleep when I see him these days. Two men
lift him in a wheelchair outside the house:
the wind or some force turns the airborne wheels.
That sleeveless jumper, collar and Labour Club tie,
dark round the jowls though just wet-shaved, it's him,
Ray Reardon hair and smile, the waxworks gazing
wherever they point him, jostled, into a van.

There's a full moon in the corridor. I put on
the glasses I don't yet need to read
the flowering seas, a couple of which he's named,
who in this life couldn't read, no one ever
having taught him or taught him he could learn.
I don't remember anyone hugging him,
no one ever I think even held his hand,
even at the end. Pneumonia, the old man's friend.
He was my brother and my friend. And not old
or not to me. Now I go back to see him,
he closes his book no wiser and no less wise.

Bluebell Wood

We're no gardeners, me even less so,
going at our bindweed and stinging nettle,
the egg yolk suns of dandelions; till here,
in May, the lovely violet blush
of bluebells no one planted. Bluebells
to bring back in their gouache mist
me and the dog, running, clodded furrows
giving way to Dumble Wood, and then the track

like a funnel into Bluebell Wood, in that
proud Harriers vest, where we'd turn
in a curve for home through the lilac dusk
of harebell, wild hyacinth, wood hyacinth,
the furthest I'd been alone, me and the dog,
out to an Arctic Circle or Timbuctoo
that everybody knew: 'You've been up Bluebell Wood?'

Then one year it was gone, just like that,
for a link road ten minutes quicker
to Mum's, to Tony's, to see Mick or Donald,
all of them, Auntie Olive, our Cynth, our Joss.
Bluebell Wood, right here, across the decades
of our garden, packed tight, and in among
is Dad, though he knew better, singing that
Bluebells are bluebells are blue bells are blue.

The Day He Met His Wife

She said goodbye to common sense
and so they booked a room
in an afternoon hotel to holiday
with fecklessness in laundered sheets;
and there was an orchid
and a crisp new paperback,
the art gallery on a working day,
a second bottle opened and a third
knowing tomorrow in twenty years
they'd wake with such a head,
a sink full of pots, the fridge
empty as Antarctica
and everything uphill again
in rain you could canoe
the middle of the street down,
which they did.

Stepladder

Built and bought to wallpaper with
and stand four-square sturdy while I change
a bulb or fit some blinds, it mostly leans
on hind legs into bookshelves in this high room,
Hamson, Hanff, and the whole gamut of Hardy,
Desperate Remedies to *Jude the Obscure*.
Every so often I climb among the summer
I spent in Wessex and blow the dust
off a page or two of then, plugged in to Santana
and him at midnight bowing it higher.
I stood there an hour the other day lost
at the ceiling on Egdon Heath,
the boy I was, while my tea went cold;
and though this morning I'm only here
to start again on the kitchen, who could resist
those four treads up to step back in time
with the reddleman and Eustacia Vye.

My Brother's Vespa

Red, scarlet even, it meant fun
and something more, stylish, Italian
on a stand, in the yard. The chrome
shone, the handlegrips revved
to Skegness in my head, my hair
a quiff I wanted to dye black, for him
not Elvis – he was Elvis. When he
climbed a ladder to the moon
on the roof for my ball he was a hero
like the pictures he took me to.
He could live forever.
He did. First we live
then we remember.

Autumn Term

You couldn't call it grief, but it's something
to not hug, just smile by the stairs to Y6,
and retrace my steps across the hopscotch.
I don't stop to not see her in Miss Duke's
magic cave of a room, whose tables and chairs
made a giant of me on open-door Thursdays,
when we snuggled together in picturebooks
more colourful than life can stay. No, I walk on.
But even so, and though it's coming on to rain,
I detour through the park, to maunder down days
when the tall-tall slide and climbing frame
were terrifying though she mustn't know;
and find myself beneath the leaky umbrella
of an oak, late for work, while the brilliant leaves
let go and fall slowly like stones through water,
so lovely, despite me, I should laugh at myself,
the picture of misery; but I don't.

Keymarkets

It was day-in day-out with no natural light,
the winter they rationed butter and eggs
(strikes; the three day week), and it paid peanuts.
But even so, despite the aisle on endless aisle
of pricing and facing tins and jars, and despite
the late hours in the warehouse, it was just
the best of times. One night we climbed
the stacked cases me and my best mate to sit
above the shift with cans of continental lager
high among the iron rafters. There was a party
at a girl's and Lindisfarne's *Nicely Out Of Tune*
to take to it – and though years later they pumped
my stomach because of her, what matters is
nobody missed us or happened to look up
between clocking-in and our stint last thing
horsing with the cardboard bailer. Canada,
he lives now, and I of course live here,
though in many ways we're still up there. Cheers.

I used to faint

I used to faint at the sight of blood.
That cauldron of early teens, even the idea
of blood and the thought of fainting
brought the self-conscious beating
in my ears, gripping my throat,
so that I almost literally died
of embarrassment. Being grown up
was an age away and was not waking
but coming a long way back
to their faces – every time, even at home,
with the same empty-headed 'Where am I?'
that they couldn't help smiling at.
It surprised me last week, a test
for the diabetes that killed my brother,
to pass out. It was just as far
and humiliating to be no age at all, my body
knowing better than me its own mind,
and it was just as bewildering
where I came back to.

Moon

We stayed up late in the old house
and when we somehow turned to talking
about the moon landing
more than a decade before you were born
we stood in the doorway
to look at it
yellow as sand through trees
by the spire at St Aidan's.
Impossible to believe
that people stood there
and looked back.
Impossible to believe,
actually, how soon you've grown.
To you, naturally,
even a dozen years
before you were born
is ancient history,
though to me a moon landing
still seems like the future.

Petar K, 1957–2007

Despite misreading a bend and coming to
in a field you thought was death but was only
your helmet jammed over your eyes, and laughing
that laugh of yours despite the pain, you were soon
out again testing the endless flat A-roads of Lincolnshire.
I think that's how it always was, and so it's him, not you,
I feel for, who turned unaccountably in front
of your sixty miles an hour. And what I want to say
from my life, my heated seats Volvo,
I want to say it's too long now, and though it's great
you liked your funeral, packed out the doors, and bringing
the sun in, *Always look on the bright side of life*,
listen, Petar, isn't it time you came back? The roads
are still there with their danger right across the fens if you like,
all those roads a sea dried between islands forever
all that sea really road after road between spires,
change down for the level crossing, the patient
speed-limit in and out of a sleepy village, then go,
open her up, letting all our schoolboy years fall behind.

Croft Juniors

is a playground I stand looking out at, forty years;
empty tarmac, the long minutes before morning break.
A cat crosses it. Then the caretaker, nameless now;
and Mr Shooter, the head, still with a rack of canes –
likewise our teacher, Mr Alsop, would use the side of a ruler,
no nonsense in his class. I can taste the texture
of penny wafers, and open my orange RE book at Moses;
toy-size bottles of milk are warming by a radiator,
and I can still smell the toilets (a wall outside to compete on),
still hear us dancing in pumps to a Dansette in the hall.
I remember match-day, longing for the bell,
the boxes of kit, one with 'sox' on it, and the jerseys,
bright yellow cotton, white button collars, though mine
was moss green. I remember diving and Mr Shooter
shouting from the touchline, even after all this time
no idea who I am, 'Well saved, goalkeeper.'

Instead of going to work

Instead of going to work I read a book.
I wasn't ill or particularly tired, there was
nothing at work I wanted to avoid, it wasn't
the sort of book you stay off work to read;
but even so I didn't go to work. Instead
I mowed the lawn, as if that was work, too damp
between drizzle, then sat with a cup of tea
and went on with the sort of book you put down
and never finish. I did the kitchen window,
as if that was work, then opened some soup
for lunch with the radio I didn't listen to,
and thought of a drive or a walk, the museum,
but instead I ironed a shirt and pottered round
on the piano, as if that was work, and had
the house to myself, talking to the cat and listening
to the rain, a real downpour, and tried not to feel
I should be doing more with the day
than the nothing I did instead of going to work.

My Town

I don't bother trying to find it, it's not there,
a sixties precinct with Keymarkets and Syd Booth's Records,
a dozen bakers diabetes fat determined women
wiry mining-stock men (though my family
were hosiery and Metal Box), and windy market awnings
that tipped rain on you. For passport
a squeaky seventies library, glass and spiral steps
and a girl like my wife crossing the bus station
biting into a green apple, all style, grace, so that
I lived through her by the window of 821
with Milton and Robert Frost; the smell of polish;
just the idea of books (I could barely read,
always getting myself in the way); and Harvest,
the spyglass guest at the feast. But colourless I think
and the accent ugly. So why is it that miles from, years
from that town, hearing it I lie down in its warmth
somewhere off Portland Square, by the Kings Bingo mum
comes out of with her tartan wheelie-bag,
I lie there as if fallen a long way: drawn round
with chalk or magic marker maybe, another
piece of evidence essentially.
How would I know? Why should I care?
The Zombies sang that then
and they're still singing it.

The Night Is Young

I have drunk
a highland malt that took my head off
to show willing at two in the morning,
the odd glass of red with a meal for my heart
and a pint of shandy at the quiz,
but not
let my hair down sick as a dog
hair of the dog, not *drunk* drunk,
not for years, and even then, hormones
everywhere, never lost it completely
brought back a curry in a taxi
on a girlfriend, not said
what I didn't know I meant *it was*
the drink talking
not Friday night drunk or office party
drunk in charge of a photocopier
let's have some fun
as Jane Austen said
on this reckless planet.

God help me to get to this age
and never *what a great night that was*
if only I could remember it
completely and utterly
drunk? me? Not ever,

not yet.

Index of Titles and First Lines

Titles in italic